Songs for Schizoid Siblings
Lionel Ziprin

Introduction, Notes, and Bibliography by Philip Smith

The Song Cave

Published by The Song Cave
www.the-song-cave.com
© 2017 The Lionel Ziprin Archive
Introduction © 2017 Philip Smith
Cover photograph © 2017 The Lionel Ziprin Archive
Design and layout by Mary Austin Speaker

ISBN: 978-0-9967786-8-8
Library of Congress Control Number: 2017941858

FIRST EDITION

TABLE OF CONTENTS

INTRODUCTION

At a remove of six decades, the emergence of a previously unpublished poem series written in 1958 by an obscure 34-year-old author who was an enthusiast of jazz and marijuana, a brilliant parodist of conventional thought forms and modes of expression, a mystic steeped in actualized esoteric insights rooted in an exotic and particular familial lineage, and a wildly creative artist at the center of the center of the underground scene on New York City's Lower East Side at its inception, might be viewed as a fortuitous reification and fleshing of the familiar "Beat Generation" narrative. Except that it isn't. Lionel Ziprin was unique in a unique way, ahead of and beneath his era. As he recalled in 2001: "I was never a Beatnik. I was never part of that. I was anti everything everybody was for."

Songs for Schizoid Siblings, a series of nearly three hundred poems linked in tone and theme, was composed for the fifth birthday of Lionel's eldest son, Leigh, on November 8, 1958. Ziprin later claimed to have written the work in "a couple of days," though it is certainly possible that in places it incorporated existing elements, given its stylistic range. The typewritten manuscript is housed in a thick fabric binder—once gray or green and now soiled and yellowed with time to an indefinite hue—on which are written the title and the attribution "by Mother Duece" [*sic*], along with a whimsical illustration somewhat in the style of Edward Lear.

Lear's shade is one of several presiding over the work. It has many echoes of the traditional English children's verses ascribed to Mother Goose, and demonstrates a clear awareness of the nonsense poetry of Lear and the sentimental retrospection of *A Child's Garden of Verses* by Robert Louis Stevenson. The overarching spirit of William Blake, especially the Blake of the *Songs of Innocence and of Experience,* is a felt presence as well, and there are parallels, conscious or otherwise, with the intricate rhythms of Dr. Seuss, whose career was then peaking notably, with *How the Grinch Stole Christmas, Yertle the Turtle,* and *The Cat in the Hat* and its sequel all published in 1957–58.

Ziprin read these poems to his children—a second son, Noah, had been born earlier in 1958, and daughters Zia and Dana would follow—and many of them explicitly address the concerns and feelings of childhood. They are, most of them, written in a playful and engaging style that has a perennial youthful appeal. But that is only one aspect of the work.

In the earlier part of the decade, Ziprin and his wife Joanne (a formidable presence and a talented artist in her own right), who had married in 1950, founded and operated Inkweed Studios, a pioneer developer of "studio" greeting cards, which transitioned the medium away from the generally saccharine drift of its chromolithographed roots into a sharper, hipper mode of knowing humor. In what retrospectively presents itself as a compellingly bizarre cultural watershed, Inkweed managed to attract to its ineffable atelier some of the most significant fine artists of the day—notably Harry Smith, Jordan Belson, and Bruce Conner, all close friends of the Ziprins—very early in their careers (Smith was on the cusp of 30, Belson a few years younger, and Conner was at first still a teenager). The illustrator

Barbara Remington—who later designed magnificent covers for the original Ballantine paperback editions of J. R. R. Tolkien and E. R. Eddison—and Joanne Ziprin herself also contributed beautiful, expertly rendered artwork to the fugitive enterprise.

Inkweed was, in business terms, a doomed undertaking, its taste and standards well beyond commercial viability: cards bearing *Amanita muscaria* jokes produced near the end of the Korean War necessarily fulfilled a higher purpose than that of goosing the market. A significant amount of money was expended by the company in an effort to capitalize on the transient 3-D motion picture and comics craze of 1953, possibly at Smith's suggestion (the artist had a few years earlier created stereoscopic artworks and an abstract short film in 3-D using a trickle of funding from the Solomon R. Guggenheim Foundation). The result for Inkweed was a series of costly and amazing 3-D cards with specially designed glasses that sank without a trace, and soon thereafter the firm was sold to an eager investor.

The greeting card medium, nonetheless, exacts a formal discipline on even the freest of spirits, and the compact phrasing and sharp conceits required for its proper execution honed in Ziprin an edgy command of the couplet and other terse modes. The lapidary concision of many of the *Songs for Schizoid Siblings* was unquestionably forged in the humbling crucible of the novelty card, tempered with a bohemian disdain for the "lust of result" that, in its immaculate trust of the moment, bears the work aloft, clear of the shallows of intentionality. The work is, in its particulars, compact, gnomic, and suitable for tribulation.

Not that this is simply an "outsider" effort of rickety giddiness.

Lionel Ziprin had been born a late Scorpio on November 20, 1924 (the same day as Benoit Mandelbrot) on the Lower East Side of Manhattan, and he lived in New York City all of his life. As the 1965 "Literary Resume" printed here as an appendix indicates, Ziprin had shown exceptional promise early on and had studied at Columbia University and at Brooklyn College. In a draft application to Columbia from April 1942, he listed literary interests, including Thomas Wolfe, Francis Bacon, Robinson Jeffers, Carl Sandburg, Edna St. Vincent Millay, Robert Frost, Arthur Waley's translations of Chinese poetry, Archibald MacLeish, Muriel Rukeyser, Greek and Roman classics, Percy Bysshe Shelley, and William Saroyan. This serious eclectic reading was furthered during his time at Brooklyn College, where he studied under Bernard Grebanier (for whom he illustrated a book jacket) and edited and contributed to little magazines. By 1949, Ziprin was producing mature poetic works of great distinction, though only a handful of periodical appearances gave wider testament to this inside narrative (known particulars are given in the Bibliography).

Despite this formal preparation, a real distinction of Lionel Ziprin's work as a whole—and of *Songs for Schizoid Siblings* in particular—is its lack of a calculated cultural or aesthetic pretense, its oracular embrace of the crafted and the immediate. It neither clamors for attention nor makes a fetish of obscurity, and it is unblemished by any positioning instinct. Its authority is of a modest and undemonstrative sort, beside which the urgently self-conscious bent utopianism of the full-throated Beat prophetic mode seems forced and culpable.

Charles Plymell observed three decades ago that "it is increasingly apparent that the Beat Generation was/is a gigantic publicity stunt masterminded by [Allen] Ginsberg," while noting how, cognate with this, the ascendant Federalist/Managerial ethos of coastal arts administration and media had inflicted a deadening sameness upon the regional diversity and local vigor of American culture and poetics, whittling its audience to a crusted nub. It is appropriate, then, that a nonconforming work such as this should be addressed to the most intimate of publics—the author's household—while bearing up, at different levels of abstraction and simultaneous resonance, a range of mundane, mythic, and metaphysical themes and concerns with inspired ambiguity and in a voice all its own. (These join at the ends, as the *domus* abstracts into the *bardo*—encircling, in a disinterested way, the *polis*—and any politics are those of causality rather than spectacle.)

This simultaneity appears largely synchronistic, though there are elements of a formal strategy: the title *Songs for Schizoid Siblings* itself, for instance, could refer to the author's two sons. It could refer to his associates (discussing Harry Smith in a 1993 interview, Ziprin commented, "Harry was a sibling, you see. He would hang around married couples. Then he would start splitting them up and making trouble."). It could be a parodic undermining of the affected tone of didactic children's literature, and of authoritarianism in general. It could refer to the "Schizoid" character type of Wilhelm Reich, corresponding to an Unwanted Child (an identity with which Ziprin is said to have had a strong identification). It could refer to the archetypal conflict of Jacob and Esau in the Book of Genesis, and its subsequent temporal manifestations. It could be an allusion to that murderous fraternal rivalry of Cain and Abel, earlier in scripture, that is mirrored in the riven human spirit. It could merely be an inspired turn of sibilant phrase. It is likely all these things.

Such a multiplicity of worlds has perceptible parallels with the visionary inclusivity of Harry Smith's 1952 *Anthology of American Folk Music,* which potentiated a folk grasp of the folk idiom through folk means. While also being a mean set of records to roam through stoned, as countless early and late adopters have discovered to universal profit. (The collector mediates the collective through the collection.) Smith's project for Folkways was assembled after he had moved to New York and was in regular contact with the Ziprins, and a large number of esoteric diagrams and sketches survive from the period, demonstrating a keen interaction between them in service of unstated, highly metaphysical ends.

Smith's studies at that time seem to have focused on an amalgam of concerns, along the lines of the Freemasonic and Theosophical eclecticism of Manly P. Hall's *An Encyclopedic Outline of Masonic, Hermetic, Qabbalistic and Rosicrucian Symbolical Philosophy* (1928), known to have been a formative influence on Smith (and many others, such as J. Allen Hynek). A natural operator in the paranormal medium, Smith employed his dazzling occultic erudition to intermittently lucrative effect with a parade of fickle patron-aspirants, including Baroness Hilla von Rebay, Andrija Puharich, and Arthur M. Young.

With Ziprin, the shoe was on the other foot, as Smith frankly acknowledged the former's superior grasp of and connections to the unknown (when not petulantly accusing him of being "constitutionally insane"). Ziprin's forebears represented a distinguished Kabbalistic lineage, and even at his most erratic, Lionel could effortlessly muster living, breathing insights and summon creative erudition in an otherworldly way. This seems to have been a family peculiarity, though the effect had been enhanced after a childhood anesthesia crisis left Lionel in a coma for 10 days. From this, his neural recovery was abetted by pediatric specialist Valentina Wasson, who later accompanied her husband, R. Gordon Wasson, on a 1955 research trip to Mexico that introduced psychedelic mushrooms to the West. (The world is bound with secret knots.)

Smith epitomized some of what he had learned from Ziprin graphically in his 1954 print *The Tree of Life in the Four Worlds*— printed by Inkweed in the unused margin of a sheet of greeting-card stock—and around this time Smith began recording a 15-LP set of Ziprin's grandfather, Rabbi Naftali Zvi Margolies Abulafia, singing and telling stories from Galilee. The rabbi died in 1955. A thousand copies of the record set were pressed but never distributed (most being destroyed in a later basement flood), and decades of overlapping efforts to secure their release have thus far proven fruitless.

The years 1954–1958 saw with the sale of Inkweed Studios; a largely abortive effort to launch a successor design company, The Haunted Inkbottle; a phase in which Ziprin apparently did editorial work for *Nugget,* an early men's magazine; the birth of the Ziprins' second son; and the inception of Qor Corporation, which Ziprin conceived as a serious firm working to exploit the possibilities of mylar-printed designs in a variety of commercial applications such as tile, fabrics, and the like. Qor created prototypes that were well ahead of their era (some have been recently adapted to designer textiles), but at the time the company failed to get traction and it fizzled slowly over a few subsequent years.

Amidst this flurry of activity, *Songs for Schizoid Siblings* managed to emerge intact, its inner keel unwarped by events. Aside from a few glancing references to topical subjects such as Sputnik, the desegregation crisis in Little Rock, and the overarching specter of thermonuclear annihilation, it is essentially a timeless work, immaculate yet fresh in its employment of language, profoundly whimsical, and structural in a manner that both reflects its Kabbalistic and folkloric antecedents and presages self-conscious literary and artistic movements to come. This is the first of Lionel Ziprin's works to be published in full, and here he himself is manifest and present with the full measure of his incarnate intelligence, responsive to the reader yet somehow always just ahead, a psyche and a potential.

The years afterward were more difficult. As documented in the Bibliography, Ziprin took up writing comic books in 1961–62, after it became clear that Qor Corporation would not be the leprechaun's bonanza it initially portended. The Seventh Street neighborhood in which the Ziprins lived, while often now viewed through a cozy glow of retrospective romance, was unquestionably becoming steadily unsuited for any kind of reasonable domestic life: entire families on the Lower East Side became strung out after a merciless criminal infrastructure began preying in earnest on the marginalized around this time, with the unwise complicity of certain ostensible agents of order and the synchronistic input of generally mounting psychic chaos. Joanne Ziprin and the children decamped for the West Coast in late 1968, never to return as a family.

Lionel Ziprin continued to write and to influence, though he gave up his infrequent public readings after a shambolic 1969 event at St. Mark's Church-in-the-Bowery in which Angus and Hetty MacLise loom large. That era saw the composition of "Sentential Metaphrastic," a monumental work of signal reputation, tantalizing excerpts of which have appeared. Ziprin began to care for his ailing mother in her East Broadway apartment, where he would live for the rest of his life. He renewed his religious practices and became more formally observant, though not exclusionary. Steadfast in place and in person through turbulent decades, he kept in touch with an esoteric network of those who continued to draw upon his limitless well of inspiration. When he died, he was buried with his ancestors in Safed, the Holy City of the Kabbalists, the highest city in Galilee and in Israel.

Songs for Schizoid Siblings

if you want

        riches and old age

do not turn

        this very first page.

s p i n d l e g
was the name of an egg
whose shell was split
in a crying fit.

square is the earth and round the sky,
and i have the ruler to prove it by.

i prefer beans
to all machines.

   machines
are not as nice
as my brown rice,
or even mice.
   machines
are not as nice
as simple ice,
or leaves, or rain,
or sugar cane.

i prefer to metal
even prickly nettle.

wake boy wake!
    we've clams to bake
    and worlds to shake!

eric invented a motionless clock
made of butterflies, wasps and bees.
the only time that it moves at all
is when he, or the kittens, sneeze.

haloo haloo,
the pigeons coo,
we've flown from france
to old peru.

exude
beatitude.

"pleasure is the measure
of all things sweet"
cried dr. eppy cureus
as he sniffed his feet.

my friend the fly
is here to spy.
he has no fear.
he comes quite near.

but i'll not swat.
he's all i've got
in proof of flies
(who in disguise)
arrive like he
(so lucidly)
and make it known
(by stance and tone)
that they come sent
from that DARK GENT.

green eyed may
       wears her new dress.
it looks like stew
       of water-cress.

lulu read a story
about a tulip which
grew all through the winter
beside an ice filled ditch.
when lulu went to fetch it
to see if it was there,
the tulip told a story
about an angry bear:
how he had kept a baby child
locked in a stony cave
and held it there full eighteen years
till it began to rave,
to rave and rant and shout and cry,
that eighteen years was long enough
to keep a baby in a cave
just made of silly stones and stuff.

sebastian bell
once tried to sell
another part to the letter L.

but brother jeff,
completely deaf,
sold it instead to the letter F.

cats are made
of light and shade.
dogs albeit
can't quite see it.

the crystal and the chandelier
are bathed in berlin's bitter beer.

the pyramid, now cold now hot,
is reduced to a lumpish dot.

the apricot, now dry now wet,
is lonely in earthless tibet.

the shoe and shoehorn that i wear
are left as relics everywhere.

the gentleman who lives next door
is sometimes friendly, sometimes sore.
he's as likely to give me a walnut sled,
as threaten to whisk me straight off to bed.

ten birds
made off with the words
that are those i cannot spell.
and a single deer
made off with the tear
that rolled off my nose and fell.
come back little deer, come back, come back,
come back with the tear you've taken,
my ears hum and my poor heart hurts,
i feel completely shaken.
and you ten birds, do come back, come back,
come back today or tomorrow,
my ears hum and my poor heart hurts,
i am in deepest sorrow.

my left eye's white
        my right eye's red
i longed last night
        for my mother's bed.

caroom, caroom,
the popguns boom,
a fire has burst in the shed.

i'm dirty with dirt
and my eyes so hurt,
and my feet drag like copper and lead.

caroom, caroom,
the popguns boom.
the hose won't work
and i've lost my broom.

i'm tired, i'm tired,
i've wrestled all day.
were school only over!....
i *so* want to play.

my dirty socks smell just like paste.
i fancy they're as foul to taste.

i climbed atop a totem pole
with seven heads and all,
thereon i found a cactus plant
just about to fall.

i picked the prickles out of it
and ate them just for fun.
the seven heads shot back in place
and seemed just ONE big ONE

i climbed another totem pole
and found a cactus too.
i peeled the skin and laid it in
a special cactus stew

the sun inside my belly slipped,
and stones began to speak.
i thought the sea above my head
had sprung a sudden leak.

i built me two houses
of copper and tin,
one for my needle
and one for my pin.

rinse your hair! rinse your hair!
soon there shan't be any there!

my brother isn't very smart.
he's very small and silly.
i wish his name were archibald.
instead of ludvig-willy.

butter the bread
upon my head.
i need it done
by half past one.

powder the bee
upon my knee.
a wind is due
at half past two.

brush the crumb
right off my thumb.
i've got to flee
by half past three.

puncture the keg
under my leg.
do it before
thirty past four.

cleanse the speck
upon my neck.
i must arrive
by half past five.

release the fly
above my thigh.
the old clock ticks
till half past six.

scrape the snow
off my big toe.
bread must leaven
just at seven.

excuse the fib
upon my rib.
i may be late
by half past eight.

let no stone rest
upon my chest.
things may be fine
by half past nine.

refreeze the air
about my hair.
it's almost when
the time is ten.

mother's just a stubborn nut,
sometimes open, sometimes shut.

the good prince of bop,
he rose to the top
through a series of odd maneuvers.
the first thing he did
was shatter the lid
of a carton of vertical louvers.
the pure light then rose
from the tip of his nose
to a spot where his bright skull pointed,
and swiftly from jars,
holding venus and mars,
he poured till the place was anointed.

the willow tree looks very sad.
is it because the tree is bad?

a is the aether that anchors the ark.

b is the blemish that brightens the bark.

c is the crimson that circuits the chance.

d is the demon that deadlocks the dance.

e is the ergot that extrudes the ear.

f is the fungus that fractures the fear.

g is the golem that gnasheth the gate.

h is the hollow that horneth the hate.

i is the ibex that invades the inn.

j is the justice that jostles the jinn.

k is the keeper that kooleth the keg.

l is the leopard that looseth the leg.

m is the matrix that mothers the moon.

n is the nadir that nurtures the noon.

o is the oblique that obverts the ounce.

p is the piston that pellets the pounce.

q is the quantum that quickens the quest.

r is the reflex that redeems the rest.

s is the solid that spinneth the swirl.

t is the toroid that truncates the twirl.

u is the unction that utters the urge.

v is the vacuum that vibrates the verge.

w is the wedding that weathers the wrecks.

x is the x-ray that xerics the x.

y is the yoga that yonis the yen.

z is the zygote that zooids the zen.

middle pillar, middle pillar,
        don't crack down,
            right and left
are the armies of the crown.

middle pillar, middle pillar
        root of fire,
            hot and cold
is the temper of your sire.

rigmarole, rigmarole,
if we don't burn wood
we'll always burn coal.

the devil
in the devil cake
refused to let the housewife bake.

the angel
in the angel food
refused to let the housewife brood.

to undo a curse
speak it in reverse!

"i'm all i have"
sobbed hungry sue.
"i wish i had
a piece of you."

the waters spin from left to right.
leviathan's curled tail is tight.
the crown below the corpus spills.
the valleys elevate the hills.
the fingers twist the eyeball in.
noah made pairs of flesh and sin.

the fire celebrates the blood.
enoch reflects upon the flood.
the goat ascends in holiness.
the duad adds to what is less.
the nostril breathes the wet brain out.
enoch lies drowned in noah's doubt.

arise
my lord.
the queen
has come
to cut
the chord
that struck
you dumb.

radiation go away
generate another day.

i'm full of hair
cried jake the bear.

i'm all remorse
cried spud the horse.

i'm bound in tape
wept john the ape.

my beak won't grow
snarled pete the crow.

they fried my lake
snapped luke the snake.

i'm rarely full
growled matt the bull.

my haunch is sore
roared rex the boar.

they've stole my beer
sniffed sue the deer.

i dislike men
hissed jane the hen.

they stole my socks
crunched mark the fox.

the buffalo
is very slow.
the yak, alack,
    also.

the battle ship
has made the trip.

methinks it's in
the captain's grip.

the birch canoe
has made it too.

methinks it's held
by spit and glue.

enough, enough
of this simple stuff.
i need things hard
like jello and lard.

don't complain, don't complain!
it's *only* a body and *only* a pain!

alas, my love,
       why
       look
       above?
the answer lies below!

why look upstairs,
       when
       such
       sweet
       airs
arise from your big toe.

the calendar tells me
        the time has come
to remove jack horners
        plum stuck thumb.

to a wedding let us go
dressed in frosting and in snow.

in which direction,
one of nine,
shall i find
my valentine?

in that direction,
one of ten,
you shall find
the best of men!

bruce, bruce
let's call a truce!
mother goose is on the loose!

i see
catastrophe.

i hear
the buzzards near.

i smell
undilute hell.

i taste
what can't be faced.

the pilgrim snapped the pilgrims' staff
first in ten parts....then in half!

the zebra
shifts from black to white.

the dragons
ostracize the light.

the sacred beasts
declare their plight.

behemoth,
love, demures to fight.

beware, beware! beware, beware!
he can shape metal out of air!

the milk is sour.
the rat's in the cheese.
i haven't the power
to split split peas.

sweet genevieve,
how she did grieve,
to hear her man
won his reprieve.

sweet juniper,
how he fooled her,
when he arrived
ensconced in myrrh.

hapless john
has homeward gone.

now i play
my own dear way.

.

the cup and saucer in the eye,
the drop of butter on my tie,
the apathetic ambulance,
the method by which wild bees dance,
the rock that keeps me underground,
the cord with which my skull is crowned,
the superannuated air,
the jug by which i grease my hair,
the thunder which my hands evoke,
the deluge in the microscope,
          are all examples of the thing
          on whose behalf my praises ring.

the alligator bound in rag,
the meaning of the mouldy hag,
the pumpkin on the pumpkin stand,
the doughnut powdered white with sand,
the pelican who feeds like blind,
the apparatus of the mind,
the names of angel and of host,
the manner by which devils boast,
the mouse who cries he's without blame,
the heel that crunches out all flame,
          are likewise aspects of the thing
          on whose behalf my praises ring.

the metamorphosis of pigs,

the man who finds what no one digs,

the spirit in the night time twitch,

the thread the seven demons stitch,

the inextensile egg of chalk,

the proclamations that i talk,

the shape of things in general,

the albatross who turns to gull,

the goose inside the blistered fig,

the cat who resurrects his wig,

the waters of the double sea,

my own unique insanity,

   are also portions of the thing,

   on whose behalf my praises ring.

```
O       LORD
            A       POT
IS      ALL
            I'VE   GOT.
```

the magic square
floats thru the air
its corners strangely round.

it pays no fare,
it has no care.
i see it as a sound.

i think i'll lead an army
across a glassy hill,
when dragons glide below it,
i'll place the order: "kill!"—

and bring me all their feathers,
and all their furry pelts,
that i might pay you for them
with alligator belts.

iggily iggily ooo
my mother's cooking stew.
when i eat it up
i'll fill my cup
with thistle down and glue.

my left shoe and my right
got switched somehow last night!

luckless paul
had it all.

let me who goes where none have went,
dissolve and pass through innocent.

there lives a man in iceland
who sports a turkish wife.
he keeps her in an igloo,
and feeds her with his life.

the strongest man in the wide wide world
just had his head from his shoulders hurled!

don't instruct by word or deed!
instruct by planting hempen seed!

put a lead ball
inside a square box,
seal it with sulphur
and thirteen locks.

open it never,
burn all the keys,
make it a throne
for the queen of the bees

wet is dry
and dry is wet
my kitten and i
are willing to bet.

white is black
and black is white.
day is as good as
the dark, dark night.

a man who rides
the lunar tides
rarely decides
on other guides.

what girls omit
is *half* of it!

i always sleep when i'm awake
        and stand when i should sit,
the candles on my birthday cake,
        burn brightest when unlit.

the reason is is when my nose
        was fastened to my face,
the hand that glued them urged i pose
        above the human race.

and so since then my body parts
are merely stitched together
by threads so weak and such fine arts
as can't withstand THIS weather.

sir julienne
on potatoes sat.
his wife
the sour cream begat.

i had a friend.
i had a friend.
his name was pembrooke pete.

i had a friend.
i had a friend,
till he moved down the street.

be sure to itemize the list
of things i don't believe exist.

the harpsichord
is falling toward
the whippoorwill's blue house.

the hangman's cord
lies round the horde
of a chipmunk and mouse.

pale, cross-bowed andrew northglow
left his footprints in the snow.
when he returned to wash them out,
he found them pools for merry trout.

aaron, aaron,
why y' tearin'
through the house today?

> i am tearin'
> cried back aaron,
> 'cause i want my way.

aaron, aaron
who y' scarin'
when y' yipp and yell?

> i am scarin'
> cried back aaron,
> heaven, me and hell.

call the doctor right away,
there are things i've got to say:
that my head is split in two,
that my fingers have the flu,
that my ears are stuffed with mud,
that the color of my blood
changes, changes constantly
like the rivers in the sea,
like the hands that cross the air,
every, every, everywhere.

i need books
and i need toys
and i need thirty sisters.

i'll stamp their toes
and tear their clothes
and give them forty blisters.

the chipmunk and the green gazelle
thought grass was something they could sell.
they carried it by bushel load
to a red lion and a toad.

the lion sniffed and smelled and roared.
the pimpled toad looked merely bored.
"no grass for us! it's much too white,"
they snickered as they shut the light.

gazelle and chipmunk very sad
agreed the grass was rather bad.
"we'll dip it in a light blue lake
and lay it on a birthday cake,

and when the parts are nicely sliced,
its layers cooled, its surface iced,
we'll take it to a chap we know
whose trade is making candles grow.

that done, we'll have a cake so rare
that should we toss it in the air,
the thing will float and rise so high
'twill pass the brightest planets by."

kerchief, kerchief
on the wall,
who's the snottiest of all?
nostril, nostril
fat and fit,
sneeze that green stuff out of it!

judgment on the world will speak
when noah grows a raven's beak.

then will a second water rise
below the world on which it lies,

as seen of course from upper skies—
at least so i, inside, surmise.

jack and jill
swallowed a pill.
they've had their fill
of empty pails,
      wails,
high hilly towns
and busted crowns.

thread the hole
        in the needle's eye.
poor men live
        and rich men die.
thread it with silver
        thread it with gold.
poor men rise
        and rich men fold.

those who blow the double horn
blew it when the horn was born.

the apple has a hole in it.
its occupant is in a fit.

so do not bite its house away.

the worm within claims he's disturbed
at having his few freedoms curbed.

i pasted horns on top of me,
and under my ten toes,
i made the sign of liberty—
to test which way wind blows.

how pure and white appears the eye
that registers the seventh sky.

four and forty hoot owls
sat on a lake,
forty-three ate bread crumbs
and one ate cake.

the bird has flown.
i'm all alone.

on either end
of the rainbow, friend,
there stands a pot of butter.

take a lump from each,
smear 'em on a peach,
toss 'em in a pan,
and watch them sputter.

sputter-butter
butter-sputter
all my toys are in a clutter.

put away your note book lad.
what's been spoken has been had.

for better or worse
let's build a hearse
of pretty sprigs and flowers.
should customers fail
we can always impale
a prince of the higher powers.

when oxen ride upon the air
they make such a stately pair.

fee fi fo fum
giants are made of maple and rum.
fum fo fi fee
midgets are made of maple and tea.

the lightwave in the vacuum flails
between the wavelength and the scales.

the chariot
is in a rut.
let's raise the beast
that drags it east.

the monad in divisive plight,
for suckling satan on its light,
split object from phenomic sight,
thereby creating day and night.

a mean and fetid bunion
crushed my only onion.

i need no bell
for this ritual.

i'll lift no rod
to call down god.

air is enough
to make this stuff.

i need no robe
to prove i'm job.

no snake will rise
between my eyes.

no simple caul
will shield king saul.

sword will not stun
armed solomon.

the laboratory in your eye
is reconditioned when you die.

who jabs a needle in his ear
the sound of number he can hear.

who punctures both his fleshy eyes
can measure what defies pure size.

who snaps his fingers one by one
can catch both hair of moon and sun.

but he who joins plain man and bull
shall earn his judgment fat and full.

the neophyte confounds the light.
the zelator confounds it more.

in the circus the clown
seems always to frown,
and never quite laugh any more.

what i feel i best do
is prepare him a stew
made of beetle and bee and boar.

the skeleton though made of many a hundred bone
is frequently, despite them all, quite quite alone.

i'll not be put upon
by *white* ceylon.
where i would swiftly get
is *black* tibet.

when at night i close my eyes
and look inside my head,
i cannot see myself at all,
or even this brass bed.

instead i see peculiar lights
that seem to dance in tune,
or little men who glide from poles
sent down from sun and moon.

they are not near, they are not far,
but seem to play some place—
four inches-in, four inches-out
of my own sleeping face.

the alphabet
within the net
is of a kind
that nets can't find.

the numeral
within the skull
is of a kind
that skulls the mind.

he who'll dance
from cork to france
will pierce his biscuit
with a lance.

don't violate
the sacred gate
or expiate
fruit adam ate.

may all who put their trust in clocks
wind up amid the timeless rocks.

tear your hair
tear your hair
it's no use!
i've listened to you
    thirteen times
and now there's no excuse.

a foot drops out of heaven.
it wears an icy shoe.
it lands upon my knee cap
and paints me darkest blue.

a hand shoots out of heaven.
it holds a burning sword.
it points straight at my belly,
and ties me up in cord.

a face floats out of heaven.
it has no eyes at all.
it crashes on my forehead,
and offers me a ball.

lo! gabriel's gold robe is torn!
the fabric's caught inside his horn!

.

earth is for mirth.
air is for care.
water's for slaughter.
fire's for hire.

what doth converge
must emerge!

i'll mend my shoes with wire
and stuff up all the holes,
and set a midnight fire
for all immortal souls.

i'll tie my hair with ribbon
and ride upon a broom,
and send my cat to fetch me
a beautiful new groom.

he will tend the fire,
and he will feed the cat,
and when i pay him visit,
be ready, ripe and fat.

i'll put him in a kettle
with cinnamon and salt,
and stir his bones to putty,
and mix him to a malt.

then i'll pour him in a glass,
and sell him at the FAIR,
to anyone who'll vow to drink
the man who isn't there.

where do i travel when i sleep?
were you to know methinks you'd weep!

salute   salute
the butter boot
that sports a butter heel,

and let's march up
the butter cup
sustained by breaded veal.

dear love, may i give you sweetmeats to cure,
all that's uncertain and all that's unsure?

beat the yolk of a greengage egg
thrice around with a chicken leg.

boil it in lemon and hickory cream,
serve it to those who scratch and scream.

he who breaks his brother's arm,
eludes him of his chance to harm.

i reach for a peach
and what do i find?

       a bushel of grapes
       and a window blind.

i reach for a plum
and what do i get?

       a box of confetti
       all soggy and wet.

i reach for a pear
and what do i catch?

       a spectacled hen
       whose egg won't hatch.

i reach for a fig
and what comes my way?

       a sad alligator
       who won't even play.

when priapus starts to moan
everybody holds his own.

it was early in the morning
when the caterpillar said
> there's a rumor that an earth worm
> can revivify the dead.

it was later in the evening
when the butterflies appraised
> the alignment of the serpent
> in the bodies he had raised.

if thee alas i must execute,
would'st mind if i employ the boot?

shall we, love, go arm in arm,
nostrils lifted in alarm?

rotation evergreens the milk
i suckle on kentucky silk.
the minimum is ten or free.
i climb a cabbalistic tree.

between my legs colossi stand.
the ogress has grown out of hand.
my teeth are scattered in the wind.
they say my brother's brother sinned.

i make confession like a sage.
i think i've reached the other page.
the pyramid is a machine.
its apex is on what i wean.

the kali yuga thinks it's past.
i doubt that light is quite so fast.
methinks i've had enough of it.
the shadows thrive in joseph's pit.

rotation evergreens the milk.
i am a member of an ilk.
i hold a card that proves i'm one.
what i project cannot be done.

☛

so take this head and beat it still.
the pharaoh king dreams joseph's will.
let's make a box to bury him.
the light in egypt has grown dim.

perhaps tomorrow will be best.
i'll bleed my doors at god's behest.
the rent i think is still unpaid.
we'll not regret i hadn't stayed.

between my legs colossi stand.
the super ego's out of hand.
jerusalem inside my eye
bids me bid egypt fond goodbye.

my little finger bleeds
pomegranate seeds.
i'll plant them in a garden
of very perfect deeds.

don't slice my potato pie.
if slice you must slice my third eye.

the asphodel
refused to smell.

the bumblebee
refused to flee.

the cormorant
refused to rant.

the dodo bird
would not be heard.

the elephant
replied: i can't.

the fricassee
turned pure puree.

the gyroscope
ensnared its rope.

the halibut
kept to its rut.

the italic
refused to stick.

the jubilee
spread confetti.

the kangaroo
refused the zoo.

the leprechaun
would not be born.

the moabite
sought a new rite.

the new nutmeg
sought a new peg.

the ocelot
dug his own plot.

the pure peacock
split its own rock.

the queer quixote
cried: let me rot.

the renaissance
let down pants.

☞

the sixpenny
slipped on its knee.

the tourniquet
gnarled deep in debt.

the unguent
detained its scent.

the vexed vortex
wove a new hex.

the whippoorwill
sundered its hill.

but young yorick
confessed his trick

to zoned zero....
who claimed to know.

i tried wisteria
   in old samaria
but found iberia
   the proper area.

the little king
refused to sing
the song that he was taught.
instead he sang
the common slang
the which his heart had caught.

apples start by being green
and end by being red.
though i rise early sunset
by sunrise i'm in bed.

i will labor with my sabre.
i will dally with my sally.
i will venture with debenture.
i will hurry with my surrey.

via the *edge*
comes all knowledge.

a scientific satellite
let's send up to the moon
to photograph what's left down here
of the remaining ruin.

the wig i wear
is rather bare.

                  it has no hair.
it's pure bald skull
and somewhat dull.

                  i think i'll tear
the thing in two,
and start anew.

the loaf's located in the crumb.
return to where you started from.
reverse directions and you find
the inner edge of outer mind.

ooo   dle   ee
ooo   dle   ow
i've purchased me a sundered cow.
its milks are made
of the seed i laid
in the path of my oxless plough.

be zealous sweet zoologist,
you are the link the monkey missed.

you magnify
things you defy.
you engender
the offender.
your defection
breaks connection.
your resistance
creates distance.

my cranium
holds twice the sum
of any brain invented.
my vertebrae,
some doctors say,
are equally indented.

the peanut on the peanut   tree
twisted till the nut was   free.

the pit inside the pear tree   though
fell and twisted straight   below.

the moral of the story   is
what's twisted hers has twisted   his.

there

is

a

place

deep

deep

in

hell

re served

for

things

that

will

not

jell

ippity clippity
my friend lippity
walked up the side of a wall.

dippity slippity
my friend flippity
slid down the edge of a ball.

the serpents' teeth are vegetable
just wax the horns of bat and bull.

of gauze the flame of flaming swords.
mere optic spots all locust hordes.

white shoes
black shoes
olive shoes
brown.
four feet of octopus
can make a man drown.

brown shoes
olive shoes
black shoes
white.
four feet of ribbon
can bind a woman tight.

the gentle wind glides down from spain.
the smell it bears gives me a pain.

the gentle wind of little rock
as well effects a nasal block.

on monday night
i solemnly dream
of apricots and sour cream.
on tuesday night
i dream, i believe,
of fingers that both sew and weave.
on wednesdays though
i dream (when it comes)
of alphabets and magic sums.
on thursdays
(when i dream at all)
i dream of spheres that will not fall...

but on friday night,
(when i fall back)
i dream i've dropped
like a hashish sack.

      and on saturdays too
      when I close both eyes
      I seem to see in blunt disguise
      that person *IMPOSSIBLE* to recognize.

magic, magic, on the wall,
press me short and press me tall.
in your service i would fall,
cubicular or as a ball.

i have a fly,
his name is pete,
his skinny legs
are incomplete.
he needs one more
and he'll have four.

were i sure that i'd live twice
i'd stop taking your advice.

scatologic
is my mind.
it seeketh out
the cause behind.

the body is the architect
of everything men must erect.

whatever is built of stone and mud
was built before of bone and blood.

first i'll draw a circle
and fill it up with dots.
then paint my mother's only skirt
with nine and ninety spots.

my dominion, short and sweet,
looms from pitt to essex street.

remember me?

        i'm in the ground.

        you saw me wag

        at the dog pound.

remember her?

        her head was found.

        now watch the cat

        roll it around.

remember us?

        we're made of sound.

        a rumor claims

        our tongues are bound.

hands off!
don't pull!
the water's full!
remove that greasy tentacle.

feet in!
don't fear!
the mountain's near!
retrace noah's fishy career.

take it away,
take it away,
what isn't tomorrow
is yesterday.

shall i invoke
the coals i poke?
shall i predict
that i've been kicked?
shall i divine
agrippa's sign?
shall i deflect
the bon po sect?
shall i surmise
jehovah's size?
shall i divulge
the place i bulge?
shall i infer
what's wigging her?

buy a chair
     and mend a table,
catch a fact,
     and write a fable.

almost all lies
are pocket size.

1.	11.	111.	1111.
said	"measure	said	"what
mr.	me	mrs.	isn't
thin	a	fat	there
to	pound	to	has
mrs.	of	mr.	never
fat,	that."	thin,	been."

slay that serpent with your eggs!
pelt him till he shows his legs!

the lad who rides alone is one
who'll find the lady on the sun.
when caught, inside that black balloon,
he'll place her back upon the moon.

i told a fib
i told a fib
i'll tell it once again.

i broke my rib
i broke my rib
by adding why to when.

i flipped my lid
i flipped my lid
by thinking now was then.

i turn the dial to channel one.
i see a serpent in the sun.
he drops, and when his dropping's done,
he claims the fall was just for fun.

let me no holy point
                anoint.
let me no holy line
                divine.
let me no holy plane
                disdain.

kissing fish was a habit
enjoyed by a rabbit
whose fur was a kind of fin.

he would look at the water
convinced that his daughter
was either without or within.

a horse's legs are four
because he labors more.

a rooster's legs are two
because his works are few.

a fish has none at all
because his life's a ball.

relax the ax
dear messrs. pax.

the leprechaun,
though irish born,
sports a green horn
somewhat forlorn.

where penguin amid cacti sleep
and wild hyena quake and weep,
where angels shaped of gray cement
rent rooms in a brick tenement,

where buffalo are high as fleas,
and coffee-stalks sprout pink green peas,
where daytime's made of ruby light
and leftward roads lead into right,

is where, if i had but the coin,
i would my body's body join,
and serve until my breath at last
confounds the present with the past.

suspension seems my natural state.
it keeps me early when i'm late.
it is indeed my only role.
through it i'm free of either pole.

pinocchio was boiled in snow.
rapunzel too with heat turned blue.

square box,
square box,
on thee i do place a pox!

said the wee lambkin caught
in the dog catchers' pound,
i prefer being lost
than i do being found.

the rings that run through oxen nose
are part authentic and part pose.

go lovely rose,
recork the hose!
the garden's wet.
the sun has set.
the lizard's dead.
the ghosts are fed.
go, go, pink thing.
the queen is king!

beware of him! beware of him!
a pin point is his outmost rim.

goodbye daddy,
it's much too late.
the law's asleep,
and i've gone straight.

the bones of the universe,
all dried up,
were laid in a hearse
shaped like a cup.

the bones of the devil-king,
clear as glass,
were strewn in a ring
none could pass.

but my bones and yours,
water-wet,
will reign when it pours
tenfold debt.

the element i can't invent
is what equates the gold i've spent.

let's catch beetle in the wood, my dear.
i've neither a net nor an ounce of fear.
let's find the giant oxen, love.
i'll wear lead-thick boots and a ten-pound glove.

peculiar pellegrini punched
the man who served him where he lunched.

sir abelard
grew round and hard
and posed for a
square greeting card.

he posed as a
lost mare at play
whose hoofs were tarred
on christmas day.

(this pose, he said
i learned whilst dead.)

sir abelard
called out the guard
when he was caught
in his back yard.

(since then, said he,
the mare did flee,

and i alone
am left to send
the greeting strung
from end to end.)

therefore, he cried
i'll no more pose
for christmas in
my toeless hose.

if pose i must
i'll do it for
the mule my mare
is looking for.

i do not always know, cried ben,
the color of my speckled hen.
instead, sometimes such sparks i see,
they blind, and badly frighten me.

the answer to the universe
lies in mother's empty purse.

i am adept....at everything inept.
i can lay bare....the ectoplasmic air.
i reassign....the order of the nine.
i violate....the third and second gate.
i rectify....the middle of the eye.
i dip my head....in ichor thrice a day.
i am chagrined....at being made of clay.

the loosest plasma
invocates
the tightest hinges
at the gates.

guide me to the darkest place.
i'd love to meet her face to face.
i know if she dwells anywhere,
she dwells, like i dwell, only there.

sun scorched pete
ate no meat.
neither did his daughter.
they fought, contrived,
but death arrived,
and flushed both down with water.

goof ball   goof ball
let's glide down a polished hall.

kool kat   kool kat
let's glide up a polished bat.

sky's a skin
so onion thin,
from it must seep
the stuff i weep.

reverberate,
dear busted gate,
and tell your broken story:
how very late
one night your fate
unsealed your hingeless glory.
reverberate, reverberate,
there shall be another date.
you'll be given chance to mend
the beginning at your end.

the inferential avenue
now calculates what time the jew
will tip his cap and bid adieu.
his fate somehow you see is tied
to what the cap holds down inside.

photoelastic
analysis
is the primal plastic
of paralysis.

let's make   a wish:
you turn worm and i'll turn fish.

in india the shadows crawl
between the cobra and the ball.
in china, though, the light is made
of cobras who exude pure jade.
however there in black tibet
a cobra lives who shirks all debt.

arise arise
i've lost the prize
that i had hoped to win.

i lost it by
a heavy sigh
conceived in heavy sin.

the sweetest calf you ever saw
was cut in half by maw and paw.

the skeleton suspends the sun
between its heart and chin-point.

a scorpion, its game is won,
when it decides to pin-point.

when psychopompus
bust his compass,
the boob of ruses
blew his fuses.

cried the bald monk:
"god's ship is sunk.
let's skin the skunk
who caused this funk."

cried buddha back:
"i have the knack.
his head we'll hack.
have you the sack?"

the demarcation of my soul
has been consigned to a mere scroll,

so mere, the thing cannot unroll
its left hand from its right hand pole.

what the devil,
what the deuce!
snakes have eyes
and so have moose.

i think i often look for things
that disinfect what in me sings.

are there many days to go?

                i think yes and i think no!

can a hand their number count?

                that depends on the amount!

there is nothing left
in the kitchen
excepting milk and bread.
i think i'll catch a spider
and pump him full of lead.

the pattern of diffraction spins
the light absorbed by inner sins.

mad rosmarie
sugared her tea
with the fin of a whale
and the head of a flea.

my favorite restorative
is dying when i really live.

my favorite hypothesis
is hitting when i really miss.

my favorite redundancy
is standing when i really flee.

the pedigree
of kitten three
extends unto
the dead sea too.

let me through glassy mountains pierce
the snake within who smells so fierce.

let me through crystal cities smash
the phoenix now reduced to ash.

let me through frozen fires thrust
the javelin made of adam's dust.

to photograph
the golden calf
you laugh
and slice the lens in half.

the winds blow
yes and *no!*

were i not a fool
would i be in school?

he who bends the inner ear
bends it out of inner fear.

he who wets the wet third eye
wets it when the others dry.

let's cut
the nut!

my aim's to grease the wheel
between pumpkin and peel.

what is before
and what's behind
hardens the core
of the undefined.

what is above
and what's below
augments the store
of all i don't know.

the hand of glory lights upon
the people permanently *gone.*

she hated it so,
she threatened to go,
and fled up the stem of a rose.

to remedy that
he laid her out flat
on the bridge of a red whale's nose.

gentle, gentle little lamb
even you'll become a ram.

the albatross
now fine, now coarse
revealed himself
as half a horse.

cut the cake, cut the cake, roland dear,
dip it in egg yolk and fry it in beer.

should a spider jump out,
don't let silly fright,
convince you that day time
is in reverse at night.

fry it instead.   dip it in egg.
for every five fingers there's one more leg.

i see a door
        cut in four.
i see a sea
        split in three.
i see what's new
        sliced in two.
i see giraffe
        cracked in half.

corn is corn
and wheat is wheat.
wolverin growl
and lambkins bleat.

mellifluous the strontium falls
in bitzy bursts of astral balls.

bananas, bananas,
yellow and gold,
those not rotten
are always sold.

the moon will ruin
the solar tune.
the sun will split
the moon's orbit.
jupiter
will saturn crack,
and bounce
sweet venus off her track.
but pluto soon
and dry neptune
will enervate
the earthen state
and rectify
the martian eye
through which,
like pitch,
a quadrate light
will burst—
and make uranus shatter first.

inside the crystal ball i see
the shaky letters I and T.

i entered the cube
through a vacuum tube.

now, all electronic,
i vie for the conic.

the mirror is my truest friend.
it proves my worth from either end.

i bucked
the holy viaduct.
in recompense
it ripped my fence.

the prince was in his counting house,
counting all his thistles,
along came father ifandbut
loaded down with missiles,
missiles to slay ducks and drakes,
dragon flies and mushrooms too,
missiles armed with reverse breaks,
just in case the time is due.

hickory, dickory duck,
the mouse ran out of luck.

doubtlessly
i'll never see
the frightful flea
who bites at me.

the color of my blood is green...
a fact observed whenever seen.

what elevates the iron gates
and sets them inside out?
what regulates the iron fates
to sympathy or doubt?

the answer
i think lies in what
the key hole
from the key ring got.

lunge inside the smallest point.
when you reach the elbow joint

that connects it with the sun,
shatter it! you've just begun!

taking rays from moon and mars,
each criss-crossed in astral bars,

split the point again in nine,
turning it to a straight line.

then, by making fire cold,
thread the line through molten gold,

and set it on the other side
of the ray you mean to hide.

this may give you space to see
the face inside eternity.

anxiety's
a saltless sea.
let's serve it at
next tuesday's tea.

zero, zero,
you're no hero.

what does it mean
when red men say
the light is shorter than the day?

what does it mean
when black men warn
the stalk is outweighed by the corn?

what does it mean
when brown men plead
the equity of things that bleed?

what does it mean?
what does it mean?

what does it mean
when one bleached drum
inveighs against the whole spectrum?

the seven seas are really one.
all are poured from the single sun.

the cow that sleeps on my father's road
is friend to an impossible toad.
together they plan to drain the well
in which my mother's thermometer fell.

the raven and   the lapwing sit

each in a fit

each
beak
to
beak.

the dragon and   the unicorn

each badly torn

each
horn
to
horn

sit cheek to cheek.

would'st care   to peek?
would'st care   to spy?

what fires from their nostrils fly?

then come
come quick.

☛

                    the raven's sick.
                    the lapwing's dead.
                    and now, instead

of unicorn   and beast

                    is born

          a burning so   infused with heat

          were i a lamb, my love, i'd bleat.

          were i a ram, my love, i'd roar
                    a bird, my love, i'd soar.

lay a penny on its side,
it's good coin and bonafide.
stand it on its head or feet,
it will buy you death complete.

i'll shed my fur
for him and her
but not for you
or mrs. blue.

i'll shed my skin
for my own kin
but not for max
or mrs. flax.

i'll bust my bones
on my own stones,
but not on pete's
or mrs. sleet's.

corfu, capillary, this ibex is not merry.
these decks are what sell. go home laved lad.
                   jell that cool   pad.
there are lilacs on that dulcimer.
dress that maid in maiden fur.
my master takes his time among the fish.
        why castor shakes his slime upon a dish.
        sky castor stakes his climb upon a wish.
so: crazy daisy it's not good
to drop one's anesthetic hood   upon the sand
one oughtn't grow an inadvertent   hand.
i knew job's book was   banned.
i know why freud froze his rare thyroid   gland.
consequently
i choose to be unseen.
         what has bean   to offer   bop?
           i'm wild on   top!
i make my ovens of an oval sheen.   the cows my joseph dreams
are always   lean.   there was a time i dug
the egypt   scene.   i don't now.
i've changed my bullock for a   cow. so:
do not make me agitate monsieur.
        i am both pure and poor. i am like morning snow.
        for me will stone behemoth   blow,

as will: beliel, buriel and bialot.
chicago something's what i've got.

                                         ☛

keep clean the sacred   pot. vessels exist that paimon,
pareht, promakos, plegit, paramatus, parasur, paraseh,
platien and pachid are frightened of.
these are drums not for public use.
the beat won't coincide to the abuse.
(patid's as good as plirok.)
split the rock. reright the clock.
reright the clock corporeal!   eee all.
                              a ball is both short and small.
        (parker was heard,   thank you.)
i was made because i like the taste of dew.
it lies like linen on the brain.
a jew goes with a blotter, in a trance.
i have seen miles davis' face replete with ants.
i have seen king david make the temple dance.
i consider them as friends. they do the same somewhere with
                    bears. thelonious is paid for splitting
                    hairs. bud's wheat grows best among the
                    tares. (correlative.) the only thing
noah forgets is noah's   sieve.
something has got to   give.
                    lunocracy controls the state.
                    i vote to   amputate leviathan.
                                    azazel   won.
                                    he jumped the gun
as he collided with
        lilith.

                                                    ☛

                    she is my lady love.
                         below   above.
                         from all six sides.
               nothing this lady   hides. so:
don't rearrange the albatross. drop the sedation
in the   sauce.
sweet cocaine lil loops lost lucifer.

                    he's just for her. .. .. ..
low lirion, lo losimon, low lomiol.
i'm in a   hole.
five   times   as   six   as   that.
my   bardo   burns   with   human   fat.
there is an abyss in my house.
my sun is eaten by a mouse.
i lack
beginnings in my zodiac.
i am armed for an attack.

i slept under a fig tree
right in the open sun
and dreamt a dream i did not dream
since i was ninety-one.

scraping the floor of the ocean is fun
cried william the whiskerless scorpion.

"i've squared the circle,
i've squared the circle,"
cried uncle goose
as he pinched aunt merckle.

antiseptic carrie
felt too clean to marry.
she fled
instead
from bed to bed
vowing not to tarry
anywhere
where flesh laid bare
wasn't given crystal care.

i'll never see an angel
because they say at school
whoever sees an angel
has bust the golden rule.

1	2	3	4
conquer	conquer	conquer	conquer
the moon.	the butter.	the near	the jelly
conquer	conquer	conquer	conquer
the sun.	the bun.	the far.	the jar.

commiserate the mystic rose!
her thorns denude her of her woes!

an effulgence bathes my skull.
      the ship of state has lost its hull.
an eyeball satellites the brain.
      the ticket men have lost the train.

an effulgence bathes my nose.
      the poppies grow in martyred rows.
the mouth holds water while it lives.
      the seamen float in seasplit sieves.

an effulgence bathes my jaw.
      the pyramid's begun to thaw.
the breastplate serves a thirteenth stone.
      i'm married to the popess joan.

confetti spreads between the wind.
the milk of mothers has been thinned.
old adam's leaf must be repinned.
that primal apple blossomed skinned.

i perspire
from an inward fire.

i congeal
from an ice i feel.

a very special trumpet
is what i badly need.
then i could help the farmer
in scattering his seed.
i'd blow it in the air.
i'd blow it in the ground.
i'd blow it north,
i'd blow it south
and four times all around.

the wingy serpent spurts.
my rigid spine bone hurts.

my neck snaps. my knees bend.
i've reached the *in*side end.

the seven headed serpent leapt
from an eye that's never slept.
the eye's located in the hand
that gives the shakes to samarkand.

a scarlet woman rides around
on a beast that's heaven bound.

though she be red and it be pink
beast will rise and lady sink.

the avenue by which to go
is quickest when it's mostly slow.

someone's put a curse on me.
i can feel it in my bones.

someone's thrown me in the sea,
my nine pockets filled with stones.

let VICTORY and VALOR go
to rivers that refuse to flow.

two girls in a boat
split the salty coat
that a whale, off course,
bequeathed in remorse.

ivanhoe
refused to blow
the trumpet spread with powdered snow.

but launcelot
knew he would rot
should he refuse to make that pot.

so ivanhoe
though very slow
lit his new skull cap to a glow,

whilst launcelot,
with dreams begot,
just shivered at how hot things got.

so keep it cool round tablers all,
there lurks a square at every ball.

the dictionary
makes me merry.
it proves there's no
vocabulary.

the queen of greece
wears a double fleece
made of purple pigeon fur.

the king of spain
commands the rain
to bounce from him to her.

the space inside the doughnut is
a cousin to the soda fizz.

but space inside that outside skin
must stand divorced of kith and kin.

if not, the holy bubbles will
refuse to rise or even fill

the doughnut in whose space the glass
must crack or turn to purest gas.

sir claghorn sits among the grapes,
his face is long and sour,
his left arm on his right foot drapes,
he waits the final hour.

authority
is you and me.

in seething water i divined
the duplicate of bo-peep's mind.

by dropping in it bits of tea
methought i stirred the alchemy.

the mind however seething hot
preferred tea boiled in a tea pot.

so separating heat and wet
i equalized the double debt.

by pouring what was inside out
i stood the kettle on its spout.

bo-peep, however, a true cook,
burst, and hurled the complete book.

"a spout," she raved, "is what divides
my lunar from your solar tides.

to stand it on its edge defies
the intent of these sundered skies.

to boil correctly water must
inaugurate the source of lust.

by this at least you edify
the ointment lavished on the fly.

by this at least the tea bits fall
precisely in one's cup of gall.

this way at least can kettle feel
the fire that provides one's meal."

the chariot has lost a wheel.
the blind man sees what he can't feel.
the empress strokes the emperor.
the priestess thinks himself a her.

a man behind a mask is he
who sprinkles salt upon the sea.

★

a man behind a mask is who
sees orange in the blackest hue.

★

a man behind a mask is one
who cools his navel in the sun.

my father cracks me on the head,
my mother on the foot.
i think what's wrong with my sore tongue
is that it has no root.

let me issue a decree:
four is seven under three.

if
in
deed
the world
must
end

,
can't
i
to
it
a
left
hand
lend
?

the bicycle i ride upon
was ridden on
                by genghis khan.
the alphabet of little lies
is not the size
                i recognize.

the moon hangs twelve and sixty feet.
the moon is lower than you think.
weren't she i'm sure she'd sink,
down on fields of snow and sleet.

buildings, buildings
            everywhere,
and not a place to live.
i think i'll send my
            body's blood
through an unpunctured sieve.

or else i'll put myself inside
and stir and steam just for the ride.

the document
with king kong's seal
is much too small
to see or feel.

the document
the ant queen gives
is much too large
to equate his.

my life alas
was made a mess
in the pursuit
of happiness.

in the pursuit
of liberty
my joys, alas,
were made to flee.

south pole   north pole
          won't you join,
       i'll reward you each in coin!

north pole   south pole
          won't you meet?
       i'll conjoin you in defeat.

lion   bull   and   eagle   man
       jumped a measure none could span.
nepthys ra   and   mertys twin
       bridged it by a diaper pin.

a is the aizez that aippez the aien
b is the botry that bostry the bien
c is the cerpx that crospx the creb
d is the danew that delpew the dreb
e is the ergiv that elgoev the ehlp
f is the forue that fracru the fhlp
g is the gorut that garoot the gerd
h is the hibis that hipsus the herd
i is the irpir that ipster the iyer
j is the joruq that joureq the jyer
k is the kefup that koofap the kelf
l is the lermo that lurkmo the lelf
m is the memen that mermun the mewt
n is the nemem that nemuum the newt
o is the oural that oorall the ohrh
p is the purek that purjek the phrh
q is the qubaj that quobaj the quev
r is the renji that ronjoi the ruev
s is the sorah that sairah the soyj
t is the tarfg that torfeg the toyj
u is the ulrof that urlruf the uuux
v is the vorie that vairie the vuux
w is the wored that waaryd the wyrl
x is the xexec that xaxoic the xyrl
y is the yafob that yoferb the youz
z is the zahra that zohrha the zouz.

the road is long, my little friend,
              it has no end,
              no fore, no aft,
it's squarer than the squarest raft.
              it always drifts,
              it gives no gifts,
it sinks like any sea-chewed craft.

if you want riches and old age
never turn over this last page.

ABOUT THE TEXT

This edition of *Songs for Schizoid Siblings* has been prepared from the original typescript in the Lionel Ziprin Archive.

Orthography and punctuation have been kept as faithful as possible to the typescript, though italicization has been used in the case of underlined words, and misspellings have been corrected, as noted below (though some archaic and uncommon spellings have been retained). Line leading, somewhat irregular in the typescript, has been regularized.

Extensive reference has been made to video recordings of Ziprin reading the work and commenting on it, shot by Robert O'Haire of Straw2gold Pictures at the author's residence on March 19 and 21, 2001. Quoted comments below are taken from those recordings with gracious permission.

Poems known to have been published during the author's lifetime have also been compared with those printed appearances (detailed in the Bibliography). In general, the typescript has been given primacy as reflecting authorial intent at the time of composition.

NOTES AND AUTHOR'S COMMENTS

p. 11: *dr. eppy cureus:* Epicurus (341–270 BC), Greek philosopher and founder of Epicurianism.

p. 12: *my friend the fly:* "When I first met your mother I was victimized by the largest horse-fly I ever saw in my life. ... I was living at the time with my grandparents and mother on East Broadway. The giant horse-fly would dive-bomb me every night. Your mother offered to visit me and *get it.* But I found it dead on the floor the evening before your mother arrived."—from a postcard written by Ziprin to his son Leigh, quoted in Laurence Schwartz (ed.), *The Messiah of the Lower East Side* (n.p., 2012), p. 221.

p. 14: *lulu read a story:* This poem echoes "The Little Girl Lost" (1794) by William Blake.

p. 18: *the gentleman who lives next door:* "This is written by a girl, obviously. Some are written by boys, some about—from girls, and some are just childish: indistinguishable."—LZ (3/19/2001)

p. 23: *i climbed atop a totem pole:* "This is the peyote. ... It wasn't all that divine, that first trip. It wasn't divine at all. What could you expect? ... It was free. The government sent it to you for five dollars a bushel. ... I didn't think it was something to fool around with a lot. ... I only sent away once for it, and didn't send away again."—LZ (3/19/2001)

p. 26: *my brother isn't very smart:* "Siblings, siblings..."—LZ (3/19/2001)

p. 29: *the good prince of bop:* "I don't know, this poem never fit in here. I always felt, when I wrote it, it came from some... different."—LZ (3/19/2001)

p. 31: *a is the aether that anchors the ark:* Describing this poem's alphabetical structure, Ziprin remarked, "It's good for the Navy—a children's code." And in reference to the 24th line: "This has been bothering me for forty years, for a word that will rhyme with 'wrecks'." (3/19/2001)

p. 32: *middle pillar, middle pillar:* In the recordings, Ziprin reads this with an intonation suggestive of the "pattycake" Mother Goose rhyme.

p. 37: *enoch lies drowned in noah's doubt:* "Enoch, that's... Enochian Chess comes from that."—LZ (3/19/2001)

p. 38: *the chord:* thus in typescript. Ziprin's comment on this poem: "You should have hung out at the tonic instead." (3/19/2001)

p. 49: *bruce, bruce:* "That's to Bruce Conner, the painter." —LZ (3/19/2001)

p. 52: *the zebra:* "That's for a snob, this poem."—LZ (3/19/2001)

p. 64: *luckless paul:* "I like that one. Answer to materialism." —LZ (3/19/2001)

p. 71: *a man who rides:* "He's hooked on moonbeams." —LZ (3/19/2001)

p. 73: *the reason is is when my nose:* Thus in typescript and recording.

p. 74: *sir julienne:* "That's not a very nice poem." —LZ (3/19/2001)

p. 75: *till he moved down the street:* "I should have said 'up.' Would have been clearer what I meant."—LZ (3/19/2001)

p. 79: *aaron, aaron:* "Aaron was this little boy, who was the son of June Vega and Ferdinand Vega, who was some kind of an angel, he was from Peru. Spoke about twelve languages. And he could talk to you like things out of the Bible. ... He saw visions of all the subjects he was talking about. I was up with him for a bunch of days, on speed. He spoke so many things." —LZ (3/19/2001) Artist Fernando Vega (Max Fernando Braun, 1932–1965) died of a heroin overdose on Ibiza; his widow Janine Pommy Vega (1942–2010) went on to become an acclaimed poet. However, they did not meet until 1962, so Ziprin's remembered association appears faulty here.

p. 90: *how pure and white appears the eye:* "See, some of these are more bearable to me than they were years ago." —LZ (3/19/2001)

p. 105: *neophyte ... zelator:* These were the first two grade designations in the widely known system of the Hermetic Order of the Golden Dawn, and the terms continue to be employed by derivative organizations.

p. 108: *where I would swiftly get/is black tibet:* "Yeah, I wouldn't last long, though. Not at the age of eighty." —LZ (3/19/2001)

p. 120: *where do i travel when i sleep?:* "I think I go to all kind of hell worlds, all the time. Really. It's embarrassing." —LZ (3/19/2001)

p. 121: *sustained by breaded veal:* "Well, we have to eat something." —LZ (3/19/2001)

p. 126: *when priapus starts to moan:* "[Chuckling] This doesn't fit in a children's book. ... That's the sex god of the Romans or the Greeks." —LZ (3/19/2001)

p. 131: *jerusalem inside my eye:* "This whole thing in Jerusalem is also bugging me 24 hours a day. 'Cause there's nothing you can say. There's nothing you can say, it's so complicated. I mean, to G-d it would be nothing to make peace, He'd just have the people—don't throw rocks, don't shoot bullets, feed everybody. And keep the politicians from shouting about war." —LZ (3/19/2001)

p. 134–35: *the asphodel:* "That's an alchemical poem." —LZ (3/19/2001)

p. 141: *a scientific satellite:* The Soviet Union's launch of the first artificial Earth satellite, Sputnik 1, on October 4th, 1957, occasioned a significant political crisis (with attendant media scare) and gave a major impetus to the American space program.

p. 146: *you magnify:* "I think that was to Mrs. Ziprin." —LZ (3/19/2001)

p. 153: *the gentle wind of little rock:* This was likely inspired by the desegregation crisis at Little Rock, Arkansas, in 1957–58 (as was the contemporary Charles Mingus composition "Fables of Faubus"). "Wasn't that Little Rock something, a revolution somewhere at a college campus?"—LZ (3/21/2001)

p. 161: *from pitt to essex street:* Two streets in the Lower East Side of New York.

p. 165: *agrippa's sign:* A reference to Heinrich Cornelius Agrippa (1486–1535), author of *De occulta philosophia libri tres* ("Three Books of Occult Philosophy," 1531–33).
bon po sect: Bön is a Tibetan religious tradition, distinct from Buddhism.

p. 178: *where penguin amid cacti sleep:* "That's not a bad one."—LZ (3/21/2001)

p. 184: *go lovely rose:* An allusion to the poem "Go, Lovely Rose" by Edmund Waller (1606–1687).

p. 198: *both:* Hand-altered from the original "flesh" in typescript.

p. 205: *pure jade ... all debt:* Hand-altered from "the jade" and "the debt" in typescript.

p. 209: *psychopompus:* A guide of souls to the afterlife.

p. 230: *gentle, gentle little lamb:* "Joanne liked this one. ... Something she could tell the children, that you'll grow up." —LZ (3/21/2001)

p. 235: *strontium:* A chemical element, dangerous isotopes of which are generated by nuclear fission.

p. 237: *the moon will ruin:* "That whole thing will take about a half a second." —LZ (3/21/2001)

p. 243: *hickory, dickory duck:* The typescript includes a rough sketch of a satisfied cat licking his chops here.

p. 250: *drum:* Hand-altered from "crumb" in typescript.

p. 257–59: *beliel, buriel and bialot ... paimon ... lirion* (etc.): The unusual names in this poem reference demons who figure in the text translated as *The Book of the Sacred Magic of Abramelin the Mage* by S. L. MacGregor Mathers (London: John M. Watkins, 1898). On a related note, discussing the magical work of his friend Bill Heine (1929–2012), Ziprin commented, "Those things are true. I mean, those names didn't come from anywhere. Those demon names *are* demon names. They're really—they're true." (3/21/2001)

p. 264: *because they say at school:* "*They* say—I didn't say that."—LZ (3/21/2001)

p. 266: *woes:* Hand-altered from "clothes" in typescript.

p. 267: *popess joan:* "There was a lady pope, she was disguised as a man."— LZ (3/21/2001) (And cf. La Papesse in the Tarot de Marseille.)

p. 268: *confetti spreads between the wind:* "This is like what they do in bebop ... tricks with sounds, very delicate into that."—LZ (3/21/2001)

p. 281: *the space inside the doughnut:* In the preface to his *The Reflexive Universe* (New York: Delacorte, 1976), Arthur M. Young notes, "It was at this time that a friend, Harry Smith, reminded me of the well-known fact that the torus, or doughnut, has a unique topology, such that a map drawn on its surface requires seven colors in order for all bordering countries to be distinguished by differences in color." Ziprin: "Doughnuts? This was years before I bought a doughnut machine. I didn't know I was going into the doughnut business. ... I have no idea what that means." (3/21/2001)

p. 282: *sir claghorn:* This name echoes radio's Senator Claghorn, a recurring figure on *The Fred Allen Show* and the inspiration for the cartoon character Foghorn Leghorn.

p. 284: *in seething water i divined:* "This is sort of semi-alchemical, like a cooking process."—LZ (3/21/2001)

p. 289: *four is seven under three:* A Kabbalistic observation.

p. 297: *lion bull and eagle man:* Cf. Ezekiel chapters 1 and 10.
nepthys ra: Egyptian deities.
mertys twin: Possibly a misspelling of "murtis."

p. 298: *a is the aizez that aippez the aien:* This work, the counterpart of "a is the aether that anchors the ark" (p. 31), employs nonsensical terms that appear to have been largely dictated by vertical arrangements of letters. "This is even more complicated. ... These have no meanings."—LZ (3/21/2001)

The following is a list of presumed misspellings and orthographic irregularities tacitly corrected in this edition, as they appear in the typescript: p. 10: beautitude; 29: verticle, annointed; 55: ensconsed; 74: sir jullienne; 77: whipporwill's; 82: furface; 122: sweatmeets; 123: greegage; 127: catapillar; 134: coromant, jubillee, leprachaun; 135: torniquet, whipoor will; 173: annoint; 177: leprachaun; 180: pinnochio, rapunsel; 191: I learned, flee,); 201: Reverberate, hingless; 216: defraction; 235: melliflous; 238: crystall; 253: woulds't [x2]; 257: anasthetic; 258: frightened off, lillith; 279: prooves; 291: kahn; 298: zoyz.

Lionel Ziprin   March 10, 1965
267 East Seventh Street   Married
New York City, N.Y.   Father of Four

A Literary Resume
One Restricted to Activities in Deployment of Words

EDUCATION: Public School 147
                            Seward Park High
                            Columbia University
                            Brooklyn College
                            The New School

Evidenced no special marks of distinguishment while subject to
formal training. An inattentive student, grades were characterized
in fact by ratings distinctly sub-average.

Lucky none the less. Received at uninvited initiative of one Mark
Van Doren a scholarship to Columbia University, in consequence,
largely, to that learned doctors' wholly accidental perusal of
certain critical papers published on such dear academic subjects
as TRAGEDY AND THE GREEKS, KEATS AND KANT,
THE LAMB in TOM WOLFE, and, among others POETIC
SENTIMENTS OF CENTRAL CHINA.

Less than happy at the atmosphere exuded by Columbia grey stone, a radical switch was deemed in order. To the dismay of the Dean transfer was requested. Our capacitations for in-put were subjected instead to the facilities provided at Brooklyn College. The change proved more geographic than real. Inattention and bad grades persisted. Literary preoccupations, however, would not be mitigated. Our energies there spun largely about the editing of a bookish review accurately titled Kaleidoscope. Substituting impromptu class lectures in place of those provided by paid professorial personnel, when paid personnel were sick, like Kaleidoscope, likewise consumed endeavors and attachments extra-curricular.

Independent literary adventuring of such order showed root long prior to collegiate attendance. At fourteen edited, printed and sold at various street corners a weekly mimeographed news-letter in consequence of which (despite bankruptcy suffered in absence of competition) this humble person came surprisingly to merit the position of assistant editor to the assistant editor of The Lower East Side News. His immediate superior there, it may be noted, was one Jeremiah Kaplan, an old kindergarten and Hebrew School buddy, who now, undeviated still from his editorial course, serves as president of Macmillan's.

While cohort with Kaplan at those afternoon offices, the evenings of LZ were spent at the time in assisting one Robert Lax (New Yorker editorial associate) in the compilation of several interminable Joyce studies subsequently incorporated in any number of authoritative texts devoted to that dean of tangled letters; and, in likewise assisting one Ernesto Da Cal (now head of the Spanish and Portuguese Depts. at NYU) in a translation of Lorca and also in what then purported to become a likewise authoritative, wholly contemporary Iberian anthology of verse.

As elected V. P. of the Lower East Side Co-op (under the auspices of the Henry Street Settlement) this same humble person devoted such evenings as remained him, at the time, to the enhancement of creative theatrics at the Grand Street Playhouse, an activity that put him in common contact with such notables at first as the late William Bendix, and with such notables thereafter as Bernie Schwartz (now Tony Curtis) and finally with such sullen stars as Mr. Brando himself. As if this extra curricula activity were not enough, quite, to account for his sub average grades at daytime school, LZ's interest in the early cause of PUBLIC HOUSING, sapped many of his night hours in the ghost composing of speeches and harangues delivered at street corner rallies by spirited citizens and officials in the name of free sunlight, non-hall toilets and rat-free rooms.

Driven, however, by penurious demons, and convinced, somehow, that our earnings as a summer Catskill bus-boy would prove wholly insufficient for the nine non-summer months between, we felt compelled to prune our services social, and soon, too soon, replaced these afternoons and nights with such services as could instead earn money. Consequently while still at Brooklyn College, we labored as part time proof reader and junior copy clerk, and by some stroke of luck, after a short apprenticeship as song plugger for Bregman Vocco and Conn, found something more our meat as catalogue writer of Incunabula for "Big Ben" Rosenzweig at the City Book Auction.

Angered by his decision to tear and then sell page by page an illuminated Flemish Book of Hours, we resigned that post after one year to the day, and betook our rage instead to the offices of the National Council of Jewish Women, where, under the command of Henry Levy, we served one year, too, as assistant public relations director for a company of girls whose traditions and ideals over fifty full years of high-minded services would never, assuredly, have permitted so bookishly harrowing an act. A Purim Play composed for this organization provoked our first opportunity at having our type writer glyphs translated to radio waves!

At the height of success resignation was submitted. The transition was effect by the offer to serve as New York editor and Literary scout for Zero Press, Paris. Its expatriate editors at the time included such worthies as Paul Bowles, Gore Vidal, James Baldwin, Themistocles Hoetis, etc. We were doubly attracted to the job as a poem published by this writer in Paris through the auspices of Zero attracted an unsolicited fan letter from no less a recluse than Sir Thomas Eliot himself. With energies still available, devotions were offered as well to another literary publication issued at the time under Roger Shattuck (associate editor at Harcourt Brace) titled POETRY NEW YORK.

The preponderance of Poetics did not stop at this metropolitan juncture. Along with his fiancée (now his wife), LZ formed

Version Records, a company that in fact instituted the consequent rash of recording outfits putting out readings of contemporary verse by the very poets themselves. The abstention of Sir Money-Bags from the operation left us with an adventure admittedly incomplete. We had nonetheless under LZ directorship managed to record such other worthies as the late James Agee and the since vanished Weldon Kees. Dylan Thomas was prepared to do recordings for Version as well (and this was long prior to his subsequent fame as a vastly improved C. Laughton), but alcohol and bad temper intervened. The experience, however, was not a wasted one. The interest in "innovative sonics," predominantly verbal and recitative in character, is with us still. LZ even now gives some small portion of his time to theorizing sound-track concepts with those avant garde purist film makers to whom "image" is all and "sound" a subject of helpless neglect. Persistent consultation in sound thematics, in its technical aspects, too, is, it may be said, a persistent preoccupation of ours.

Concurrent with our cultural devotions, earning necessity provoked the following series of chores. As a member of the Newspaper Guild, we served the Jewish Telegraphic agency as a Jack of all skills. Advanced from that status to one more clearly defined, under Morton Wishengrad, at the Overseas News Agency, we became merely a news-writer whose monotonous assignments were happily sprinkled with demands for additional service as a film critic, and namely of those foreign in origin. Ascending still, but this time under Landrum Bolling at the same Agency, we served some two years as Editor for Affairs and Events Middle Eastern.

We found the news nonetheless painful—painful to gather and more painful to write. Ending our career with the Fourth Estate proved, however, a conclusion somewhat less than definitive. We still retain threads. From that day to this LZ persistently provides editorial and feature pieces for Seven Arts, a syndicate covering some 600 small town weeklies both here and abroad largely devoted to Jewish interests.

Writing as an art and as a way of earnings subsided in part after a stint of some years in the design and manufacture of greeting cards. With our wife we directed the graphic talents of a group of then gifted young men who have since almost invariably merited position of acute esteem in both the commercial and fine arts. In the latter category, notably Bruce Conner, Barbara Remington, Harry Smith, Jordan Belson, Seymour Leichman, etc. It may be added that if our pen largely rested those years, it at least found some, if limited, exercise in its responsibility for all card copy. It may be added that the card company was the very first of that order since come to be known as "studio" cards. It was, of course, nation wide in sales. The sales of the company rendered the unanticipated liberty to generate and edit NUGGET magazine anonymously, if only for nine arduous combat-scarred months.

A sudden and increased interest in commerce affected, soon afterwards, an association with a technical research group, devoted largely to advanced building materials. During those four intensive years following, our deployment of words was curtailed to Technical and Administrative reporting only. Our subsequent interest in economics and finance, although admittedly abstract in character, curtailed those literary curtailments still more. The subject matter of our endeavors being gold-concerned and monetary, security demands and multi-meaning coding requirements necessitated our reduction in literary status still further. At that point we dropped, we felt, from writer to cryptologist. And it is in this latter art that our endeavors still largely lie.

To relieve the strain of papers intended for governmental agencies and removed private banking interests, we accepted the call from Dell to assist in the development of its own comic book editorial staff. And, consequently, for what might therefore justly be called comic-relief, we concurred to create any number of properties. We were responsible for what then became and may still well be, some of the best selling titles in that field. "Combat," a series, created by us, and by us written for Dell, has since served the title and format for the hour long TV production by that same name.

Although our experience in TV has been limited, it might be said that at its inception many long years ago, during those months when channel 2 was alone in operation, we were called on to write, in behalf of both Coca Cola and General Foods the first thirteen installment children's program produced. It was titled Kabbalah the Kook.

Transcribed, with minor corrections of spelling, from a carbon-copy typescript in the Lionel Ziprin Archive.

A PRELIMINARY BIBLIOGRAPHY

Very little of Lionel Ziprin's literary work was published during his lifetime. As the 1965 "Literary Resume" presented here as an Appendix indicates, his writing was one tributary of a continual torrent of activity, much of it directed toward securing an improvised livelihood. LZ's uncredited contributions to periodicals and comic books have only begun to be investigated, and his editorial contributions to the Overseas News Agency and Seven Arts Features Syndicate, which seem to have largely entailed anonymous rewrites, are here omitted. This bibliography makes no claims to completeness and is intended as a launching place for further research into his work.

BOOKS

Lionel Ziprin, *Almost All Lies Are Pocket Size: Excerpts from the Work of Lionel Ziprin* (New York: Flockophobic Press Ltd., 1990). *A wooden box housing letterpress-printed excerpts from four of Ziprin's poetic works, accompanied by a red flexidisc (the propriety of whose color was a later concern) of LZ reading and a photograph of the author, issued in a signed and numbered edition of 350.*

Laurence Schwartz (ed.), *The Messiah of the Lower East Side* (n.p., 2012). *Collects postcard writings and correspondence from and to Ziprin, with recollections of a close friend.*

PERIODICALS AND OCCASIONAL PIECES

The Eyes of Youth (ca. spring 1937).
A mimeographed newsletter, written and illustrated by Ziprin at age 12. Priced at 2¢, it was sold by LZ on the streets of the Lower East Side.

Seward Folio (June 1940; January 1941; January 1942).
These little magazines from Seward Park High School are known to include poems by LZ, who was also apparently editor at one point.

"A Journey through Hades" in *O.K.* (ca. 1943).
This two-page spread of captioned cartoons, from a little magazine associated with Brooklyn College, prefigures the humor of the Inkweed Studios cards. Ziprin is listed on the masthead as an Associate Editor. (In the "Literary Resume" included here as an appendix, LZ also mentions being involved with a magazine called Kaleidoscope *during his time at Brooklyn College.)*

Dustwrapper illustration for Bernard D. N. Grebanier, *Mirrors of the Fire: Poems and Translations* (Boston: The Mosher Press, 1946).
This collection of writings by a prominent Brooklyn College English professor features an ink illustration by Ziprin on the dustwrapper. Three hundred copies of the edition were signed and numbered by the author.

"Math Glass" in *Zero* 2 (Summer 1949) and 3–4 (Autumn 1949–Winter 1950).
Ziprin reportedly received a complimentary letter from T. S. Eliot in response to this poem, published across two issues of a literary review edited

by his friends Albert (Asa) Benveniste and Themistocles Hoetis (George Solomos) in Paris and Tangier.

"My Art Is an Art" and "So That What We Saw" in *Poetry New York* 2 (1950).
These two poems lead off the second issue of this serious little magazine, edited by Roger Shattuck and others.

Unspecified contributions to Inkweed Studios cards (ca. 1951–54).
LZ wrote and in some cases illustrated an unspecified number of cards during the Inkweed Studios period, the compact poetics of which presaged Songs for Schizoid Siblings. *In 2016, Dust-to-Digital initiated a series of reprints of some Inkweed cards, in conjunction with the Lionel Ziprin Archive.*

Unspecified contributions to *Nugget* magazine (ca. 1956–58).
In the wake of the sale of Inkweed Studios, Ziprin was in communication with publisher Michael St. John about his fledgling men's magazine, Nugget *(most of a detailed letter LZ wrote to St. John on July 22, 1956, survives). In the "Literary Resume" printed here as an appendix, Ziprin notes that he worked on the magazine anonymously for "nine arduous combat-scarred months" around this time. A survey of issues from 1956–57 suggests that St. John did not heed Ziprin's advice to distinguish his magazine from the contagiously stolid Hefner enterprise by giving it more of a cultural and semiotic edge.*

Unspecified contributions to Qor Corporation commercial design work (ca. 1958–62).

LZ oversaw and contributed artwork to this enterprise, which was intended to market mylar-based printed designs for a range of applications. While Qor never attained commercial viability, a selection of their designs (including LZ's "Scribbles") were adapted by artist Carol Bove to a line of textiles for the Whitney Museum in 2015.

"…a work in progress …jorrin productions" in *Vision: A Journal of Film Comment,* Volume 1, Number 2 (Summer 1962).

This, the second issue of Film Comment *under its original name, begins with a three-page poem/prospectus, largely written by Ziprin, for a 35mm film collaboration with photographer Mario Jorrin ("concepted in conjunction with ziprin, ziprin and heine") entitled "operation narQo." The project appears to have been short-lived.*

"From SONGS FOR SCHIZOID SIBLINGS" in *ICA Eventsheet* (March 1970).

This calendar bulletin from London's Institute of Contemporary Arts included five poems from the series, along with an announcement that "Asa Benveniste will read and talk on the poetry of Louis Zukofsky and Lionel Ziprin on Wednesday, March 11 at 8:30 p.m."

"A Few Opening Lines from an Eleven Hundred Page Work in Progress Titled *Sentential Metaphrastic*" in Angus and Hetty MacLise

(eds.), *Aspen* 9 (*Dreamweapon/The Psychedelic Issue,* Winter/Spring 1970).
Period excess is on full display in this issue of the multimedia magazine Aspen. *An opening excerpt from "Sentential Metaphrastic" was included as a separate leaflet.*

"What This Abacus Was" in undetermined periodical (ca. early 1970s).
This hermetic poem was reportedly written ca. 1949, around the time that "Math Glass" was composed. Joanne Eashe is said to have fallen in love with the author after reading it, leading to their marriage. A tearsheet exists from its appearance in a periodical twenty or more years after its composition (possibly in the UK), but details of that publication have not been established.

"Afterword" in Derora Bernstein, *Black Bread and Tea* (Berkeley: Archangel Books, 1978).
LZ contributed a striking pendant to this collection of poems by a writer who died tragically, on the eve of her wedding, at age 31. Joanne Ziprin is acknowledged in the credits.

"From *Songs for Schizoid Siblings*" in Jeremy Rendina and Michael Klausman (eds.), *The Nightjar Review* 1 (2005).
Ziprin, the featured writer for the issue, is represented by a selection of 22 poems from the series.

"Dear Harry" in Clayton Patterson (ed.), *A Night of Art, Film, and Ultraperception* (n.p., 2006).
This magazine-format booklet issued in conjunction with a September 14, 2006, art and film program includes a three-page LZ piece, written as a letter to Harry Smith, discussing the Abulafia recordings and presenting other stray bits of information.

COMIC BOOKS

Ziprin's work as a comic book writer and editor has yet to be thoroughly investigated. It is known that he was employed at Dell Publishing Co. around 1961–62 (according to a 1966 resumé of uncertain veracity, LZ was "responsible for both comic book copy and graphic directorship of illustrators" at Dell). This was during the period that Dell's publishing partner, Western Printing, broke off to form the Gold Key imprint, taking with it the majority of the licensed properties—such as Disney and Warner Brothers titles—that had been the mainstay of the operation. Facing the departure of the majority of its publishing content, Dell was scrambling to formulate and produce new titles at the time under the editorial direction of comic book veteran Leonard "L. B." Cole (who in 1961 had been brought in to replace John Stanley, the mercurial genius behind Little Lulu). Cole left Dell in April 1962, and Ziprin's subsequent involvement with the firm is unclear: LZ later claimed that Cole's successor threw a rock the length of the Ziprin apartment while visiting, prompting Lionel's retirement from the industry.

The following titles were identified either by Ziprin or by his family members as having contributions, or are suspected to have Ziprin scripts or supplemental features, as noted. (One possible stylistic distinction of

Ziprin's writing is a frequent use of capitalized words for emphasis.)

Combat (first issue cover-dated October–November 1961, released August 1961; published until 1973, but issues after #26 [October 1967] reprint earlier content).
LZ claimed to have created and written for this title. Per his son Leigh, the Bataan Death March story in issue #3 (cover-dated March–May 1962, released December 1961) was written by Joanne Ziprin.

Voyage to the Bottom of the Sea (*Four Color* 1230, cover-dated November 1961).
Per LZ's son Leigh, this one-shot film adaptation was written by his father.

Kona, Monarch of Monster Isle (first issue published as *Four Color* 1256, cover-dated February–April 1962; 21 issues released through late 1966).
Ziprin's most sustained and noteworthy effort in the medium. LZ claimed to have conceived and written this eccentric but successful series, though it is not clear at what point his contributions ended (the initial story sequence ends with Kona *10; issues after that are believed to have been mostly scripted by prolific comics writer Paul S. Newman; writer Don Segall has also been associated with the title). Occasional references to "the Four Worlds" etc. produce a jarring effect in a caveman comic book, though the series is highly regarded by non-Kabbalists.*

87th Precinct (first issue as *Four Color* 1309, cover-dated April–June 1962, released January 1962; only two issues were published).
While no documentary evidence is known of Ziprin's involvement with

this comic-book spin-off from the TV show based on Ed McBain's crime novel series, both issues of this title bear some stylistic similarities to LZ's other comics work. Bernard Krigstein, the exceptional comic book artist who drew the first issue, described the script as "the most fantastically absurd story that has ever been typed or presented to an artist for a breakdown" in a 1962 interview with Bhob Stewart and John Benson. The second issue addressed heroin smuggling in great detail, and Krigstein withdrew from the series.

New Tales of the Wizard of Oz (unpublished proposal, ca. mid-1962).

This unrealized project created for Dell survives as a proposal and script. Perhaps inspired in concept by Dell's New Adventures of Sherlock Holmes *(two issues of which were published in 1961), Ziprin's script includes a surprisingly detailed humorous depiction of magical evocation for a child audience. Significantly, LZ claimed this project floundered the same month that Harry Smith's filmic Wizard of Oz project* (No. 13) *collapsed, possibly April 1962 (coinciding with the departure of editor Leonard Cole from Dell).*

UNPUBLISHED WORKS

Ziprin left a substantial body of unpublished writings. Following are details of those works for which specifics are known.

Numeration (1966). 55 pages.
An excerpt appeared in Almost All Lies Are Pocket Size.

Costly Postage (ca. 1969). "Thousands of pages."
Reportedly contains a diary-like account of LZ's doings following his separation from his family. Written for Joanne, it was too expensive to mail, and the still-sealed package resides in the Lionel Ziprin Archive.

Sentential Metaphrastic (1965–71). 703 pages.
LZ: "The longest, most boring poem in the English language." Brief excerpts appeared in Aspen 9 *and in* Almost All Lies Are Pocket Size.

Clues to a Scotland Yard Mystery (1987). 217 pages.
An excerpt appeared in Almost All Lies Are Pocket Size, *and a raucous videotaped reading survives (see Film Appearances section).*

Internet (ca. late 1990s). 83 pages (two columns per page).
A manuscript comprising nearly 1,500 quatrains, the first line of each being "In Internet".

FILM APPEARANCES

The following is a list of known identifiable films featuring Ziprin. Extensive unreleased video footage of LZ in later life is known to exist.

Noah on Seventh Street (dir. Laurence Schwartz, 1965).
This short film by a close friend preserves memories of the Ziprin family on the Lower East Side.

Hats (dir. Pip Benveniste, 1970).
This short film reportedly features Ziprin trying on hats.

Lionel Ziprin Murder Story #1 (dir. Clayton Patterson, 1988).
A two hour and three minute video of Ziprin reading and commenting on his Clues to a Scotland Yard Mystery.

The Book of Logic (dir. Clayton Patterson, 1989).
An epic twenty-hour video, programmed to show as a series of ten two-hour installments at Anthology Film Archives. The series was canceled after the third screening was attended only by Ziprin, Patterson, Deborah Freeman, and Ira Cohen. As described on the series poster: "Supposedly an Epistomilogic Fantasy, a pretensive exposition of Logistica-Talmudica, 'The Book of Logic', in all its multiple intricacies, is in fact a Slam-Bang Exorcists Ritual which effectively guarantees subsumation of 'All-That-Ails-Thee' and 'Peace-Everlasting' to such precious few as having the stamina to see, hear and bear it."

American Magus (dir. Paola Igliori, 2001).
This film counterpart to Paola Igliori's book on Harry Smith includes interview footage of Ziprin.

Protocols of Zion (dir. Marc Levin, 2005).
This personal documentary includes part of an interview with Ziprin.

PHOTOGRAPHS

Harvey Cohen, *The Amphetamine Manifesto* (New York: The Olympia Press, Inc., 1972).
This assemblage of writings and images from the ill-advised NYC speed scene includes a photograph taken by Don Snyder of Ziprin and Harvey Cohen reading from "Sentential Metaphrastic" at a 1969 event at St. Mark's Church in-the-Bowery. LZ later claimed that this was his last public reading.

Don Snyder, *Aquarian Odyssey* (New York: Liveright, 1979).
This matchless photographic record of the '60s counterculture by a direct participant includes a color photograph of LZ at a kitchen table.

GALLERY EXHIBITIONS

From Inkweed to Haunted Ink: The Beat Greeting Card. Curated by John McWhinnie. John McWhinnie @ Glenn Horowitz Bookseller, New York: December 14, 2011–January 21, 2012.
This was the first exhibition of greeting-card works from Inkweed Studios and its successor, The Haunted Inkbottle.

Qor Corporation: Lionel Ziprin, Harry Smith and the Inner Language of Laminates. Curated by Carol Bove and Philip Smith. Maccarone, New York: September 7–October 19, 2013.
This exhibition included prototypes and samples created for Qor Corporation products by Harry Smith, Lionel Ziprin, and others, as well

as a selection of artwork and esoteric notes and diagrams by the Ziprins and their circle from the early to mid-1950s.

SECONDARY SOURCES

Paola Igliori (ed.), *American Magus: Harry Smith a Modern Alchemist* (New York: Inanout Press, 1996).
Includes an interview with Ziprin largely focused on his relationship with Harry Smith.

John Strausbaugh, "The Rabbi's Basement Tapes" in *New York Press,* Vol. 10, No. 40 (October 1–7, 1997).
A detailed overview of the Abulafia recordings.

Jon Kalish, "High on Kabbala" in *The Jerusalem Post* (June 11, 1999).
An account of the Abulafia recordings and attempts to secure their preservation and release.

Jon Kalish, "Lower East Side Spirits," Jewish Communication Network website (March 13, 2000).
A more detailed account of the Abulafia recordings.

Romy Ashby (ed.), *Goodie Magazine* 22 (2004).
This issue of this little magazine (edited by Romy Ashby and published by Foxy Kidd) is devoted to Lionel Ziprin, with a long interview and many photos.

Jon Kalish. "A Beatnik Finds Treasure in His Grandfather's Beats" in *The Jewish Daily Forward* (January 27, 2006).
Brief article on the Abulafia recordings.

John Freeman Gill, "Giving Voice to Sacred Prayers" in *The New York Times* (February 5, 2006).
Brief article on the Abulafia recordings.

David Katz, "Angels Are Just One More Species" in *Jewish Quarterly* 204 (Winter 2006/2007).
An overview of Ziprin's life and career, with interview excerpts.

William Grimes, "Lionel Ziprin, Mystic of the Lower East Side, Dies at 84" in *The New York Times* (March 20, 2009), page A19 (New York edition).

Deborah Freeman, "A Couple of Hard Bop Holdouts, East of Eden" in Clayton Patterson (ed.), *Jews: A People's History of the Lower East Side,* Vol. 2 (New York: Clayton Books, LLC, 2012).
A detailed account of Ziprin's life written by a close friend.

Andy Battaglia, "Today is an Example" in *Frieze* 164 (June–July–August 2014).
Discusses preservation efforts surrounding Ziprin's work and effects.

ACKNOWLEDGMENTS

Lionel Ziprin, whom I was fortunate to know in his later years, made the sacrifices necessary to create and preserve this work, transmitted his matchless insights with humor and forbearance, and inspired the efforts necessary to bring it to publication.

The children of Lionel and Joanne Ziprin—Leigh, Noah, Zia, and Dana—lived this story, kept the faith, and provided memories, connections, and encouragement over many years.

Among the departed: Jordan Belson, Ira Cohen, Bruce Conner, Rosebud Feliu-Pettet, Bill Heine, Themistocles Hoetis (George Salomos), and Tom Sigman provided their memories of Lionel and Joanne Ziprin, and insights into their work. Eternal memory to them all.

Among the living: Djin Aquarian, Khem Caigan, Leyna d'Ancona, Catherine Heinrich, Paola Igliori, Aishling Labat, Kirt Markle, Jeff Maser, Clayton Patterson, Jeremy Rendina, Laurence Schwartz, Marc Silber, and Gerd Stern provided memories, research, information, insights, and introductions. Bill Schelly graciously made information available in advance of the publication of his *John Stanley: Giving Life to Little Lulu* (2017).

Carol Bove has facilitated, encouraged, and collaborated in this research and related efforts for over a decade. Without her friendship and vision this and much else would not have come to be.

Robert O'Haire of Straw2gold Pictures graciously provided access to and permission to quote from video and audio recordings he made in 1999 and 2001 of Lionel reading and commenting on his work, and reminiscing and being interviewed in a setting of trust and comfort. Without Robert's generous commitment of his time and technical expertise to Lionel, much of value would have been lost. And being able to hear Lionel once again, as in life, was of inestimable benefit.

Ben Estes and Alan Felsenthal at The Song Cave had the vision to take on this project and the intestinal fortitude to see it through a succession of suprarational delays and hollow promises that would have made a smoking, irradiated ruin of lesser enterprises. Long may they reign.

Katherine Chesney Smith has contributed to this labor through her insight, intelligence, knowledge, experience, clarity, hope, ethics, love, and attainment. I would scarcely know the meaning of these words without her.

OTHER TITLES FROM THE SONG CAVE: